Mila Sor

THE MOON IS
MY WITNESS

Edited by Gyl Carla Das

2022

The Moon is my Witness

English editor: Gyl Carla Das
Book cover design by Rasika N. Nyoman

Printed on Amazon
ISBN - 9798815850194

Third paperback edition May 2022

This book is dedicated

To those who have found the loves of their lives, and lost them,
and to those who have lost their loves and found them again,
thank you for coming along with me
on this journey of heartbreak and healing.

LOOKING FOR YOU

Looking for you in this quiet night
I crossed all bridges
and let all my lonely moments
rise up to the stars.
Looking for you
I saw the water of rivers
overflow their beds and hurry to the seas,
and the earth shook with excitement.
From the sound of footsteps I made bells
which I sent out like humble servants
to announce your absence
to the lighthouses on the shore.
I turned into water, transparent and cold
and I sent out a wave like a boat
to float away looking for you.
The tangled threads of dreams I wove into a net
and with it I caught the truth of our touch
and gave it as a gift to eternity.

WAITING FOR YOU

Waiting for you with the blades of pain
I've carved my soul in the shape of yours
and poured all my love in it.
Waiting for you I killed the talk of crickets
whose noise deafened the night
and shrunk the earth to a pea.

Waiting for you, I hid a dream in your wakened eyes;
one day it will awake and shine
like a sun being born from the womb of your land.
Saffron, white, and green
saffron, white, and green
will wave on both ends of the world.
What was farthest, my hands brought closer
what was dearest, my soul touched
waiting for you, even the unattainable will come one day.

DO YOU REMEMBER

Do you remember the time
when we felt the pain of the wilting flowers
that lay hidden within the earth,
when swarms of bees were dying for pollen and honey
and we enveloped the whole world with our joy?
Do you remember when we begged the wind
to plant us like dandelion seeds
at the same spot, again and again,
where our gazes first lost themselves in each other?
And how, overtaken by waves of love,
we swam far from the shore
and the greatness of our love could not fit
into any lifeboat we found?

O time, take me back on your wings of light,
take me back to the source of my life!
O sun, unearth the shadows of silence
and illumine them with the sound of his voice!

COME WITH ME

On the pathways of this world, I see flowers
covered in dust beside rusty railroad tracks,
I see children chasing the wind through open train car
windows,
roadside rocks measure Earth's pulse
with an outdated stethoscope,
rains fall to fill the lakes,
and tears to fill cracks in hearts.
In the churches, wax flows down crosses,
healing wounds.

And you hear my weeping in your voice.
On the altar of my heart my tears
like holy water heal the scars of love.
Come with me to that place
where birds change feathers before every flight
and the ground soaks up all the passion in the world,
come back in time with me
to that place where from the light of your love
a flower grew and married the sun.

DRIFTING APART

When the heart breaks,
the pieces are knives.
I have no pain that is not connected to you,
nor a scar your finger hasn't touched.
The rain drenching my hair
is the recycled weeping of a butterfly
dying at the end of the day.
When the heart breaks,
the epicenter of all quakes
is in our joined hands –
the tectonic plates shifting
is their drifting apart.

AUTUMN CREEPS INTO MY HEART

Autumn creeps into my heart.
The garden is dry and deserted,
and the red flowers I planted last summer
have left stains of blood.
I am bleeding. I am bleeding, don't you see?
The wounds are from your steps
when you walked out of my heart.
The wounds are from the unspoken words
that I held captive inside me.

Do you see the night creeping in?
I have left the door ajar for you,
but instead, the darkness is coming in,
filling me like deadly poison,
leaving me numb with pain.
The stars are watching me. Are they smiling at me?
They always smile.
They are happy to be friends with the night,
but not me! Not me!

The Moon is my Witness

I fear this loneliness, my dear.
Give me your hand, for together we can chase away the
night.
Together we can do it!

But you are gone,
and with you,
the dreams of my tomorrows like white clouds
sailed away from me into the unknown.
My garden is thirsty for rain.
My garden is in need of your caring hand.
Instead, I water it with tears of anguish,
and when the season comes
I will harvest the fruits of my pain.

Mila Sor

I'LL INVITE THE SUN

I'll invite the sun on my palm to set.
The day that turns to dust through the fingers,
will be sown at night by the wind
like the seed of a new reality.

My existence
will turn into a faint spark,
a single note of God's symphony of creation.

In the book of destiny, angels will pen my speech,
and my works, like well thought out chess moves,
will give rise to new constellations.

WHEN THE CITY SLEEPS

When the city sleeps,
I dream I'm a child again.
In the backyard of my father's house
as the wind whispers of broken hearts,
I bury sparrows with broken wings
I had kept in a shoebox.
Again I count the blocks in the alley cobblestone
pressed into the ground like a stamp of another time;
I measure their length in a child's hands
and trust that if I walk over them long enough,
I will arrive at the start of all that exists.

In the dark
someone reaches for the heavens
and steals the dreams of gods.
I make a gift of my own dreams to myself.
I become sky, and the city a hungry bird
who every night tries to conquer a portion of me.

WHEN THE SHADOW OVERTAKES ME

When the shadow of life begins to walk before me
I will realize the future in all its colors:
I will know when the bees return
without pollen to the hives,
when gifted flowers begin to wilt too soon,
and when migrating birds are back late from their journey.
I will know when the image
hidden in the mirror that is clouded by oblivion
distorts and flows through the glass like a stream,
and the sky opens to receive the cloud called soul.

When the shadow overtakes me,
the need to walk will perish,
and invisible steps will stop there where hope,
like a sprout with its head bowed down
penetrates the earth
and again begins growing towards the sun.

THE MOON IS A WITNESS

The words I wanted to say to you
I hid them in the dust at your doorstep.
They get a voice at night
when the bumblebees trapped in the sleeping flowers
struggle for their freedom.

The moon is a witness
to when at night the walls move,
to when small sparks enter my insides
illuminating me,
sparks that turn into suns by your touch.

Mila Sor

NAMASTE MY LOVE

Today, like an Indian dancer, I will dance
on the rainbow connecting two ends of the world.
Playfully I'll approach you
and the bells on my bare feet
will wake you from your daydreaming
and salute you: Namaste my love.

O flowers, pour your dust on my hair
so his kisses can land on it like butterflies
and grant me moments of perfection!
O destiny, build me a bridge of stars
that will carry me to the garden of joy
where the touch of two hearts will set the night on fire.

The Moon is my Witness

THERE IS NO SECRET YOU DON'T KNOW

My body is a raft anchored on the shore.
From the light around me,
shadows of clouds and splintered rocks are born,
and the smell of salt parting from the sea
sticks to my skin like pain.

Thoughts float in crystal boats with the sound of water.
Tears run down my cheeks like drops of a severed wave.

There is no secret you don't know
nor a shadow in which I could hide
your footprints in the sand.

Mila Sor

I WON'T FOLLOW YOU

An open door leads to the path
still wet from the rain long ago.
I hear your swift footsteps on it.
Not a thought, nor a look can catch up with you,
nor death that lurks at the edge of life.
The void of the look becomes the sky,
and the sigh becomes a rock
sinking
to the bottom of loneliness.
The voice of thunder announces changes
waking the roots in the ground
and the ashes in the graves.

At the open door, I stopped.
I won't follow you into infinity.
Its emptiness frightens me;
out of its bottomless depth
the night is always born.

UNSTOPPABLE DESIRES

The water from the faucet of unstoppable desires
drips into our thirsty hands, and never spills over.
Fresh and sweet is its taste on the skin,
like the memory of a first kiss.
On the banks of ancient dreams
we dig up sunken ships with remnants of the past:
a soft touch of lips, thorns of a mimosa twig,
a broken heart in a bottle that had sunk
from the weight of sadness.

We keep reaching out to each other,
losing and finding each other again,
forgetting and meeting again
as if for the first time.
Over the water our shadows intertwine
and vanish into the light of now.

WE KNOW

We know that in your chest the ocean sleeps.
In mine, the salt awakens the pain in the healed wounds.
Blood is dripping from my fingertips;
you take the drops and plant red poppies
by the path leading up to the sky.
Tread quietly on that path,
as quietly as a thought, a prayer, a secret.

When we're alone and impatient,
my world shatters like a mirror before you.
In the jagged pieces I see my hidden self.
I, I, I...
I find myself in your trembling bliss,
I grow with the tide of love in your heart,
I let out a cry when my desires
are released from fear.
I, I, I...
I lose myself in you
I am your cardiogram
writing out the language of love
when all other languages are silent.
Drop by drop I melt in your eyes
like a teardrop of joy hidden in a sleeping flower.

The Moon is my Witness

Hear my scars weeping!
Touch the softness of poppies growing
in the ruins of my shattered world!
Poppies, poppies...
their redness is blinding me!

We know how to put together the broken pieces
into a mosaic of colored pebbles,
we know that every morning
in the cracked furrows of the fields
a woman seer reads our destiny.

Mila Sor

THE BLADE OF TIME

Like the peel of an apple
life moves in a spiral.
Slowly
          we all
                    fall
                              down
                                        into the whirlpool.
On the other side of the horizon
we see every day going by,
lighting the fuse of the next one
into infinity...
The blade of time is always cold
even though like an anchor,
it is submerged into the boiling blood of life.

LONELY

I'm lonelier than a butterfly
that dies at the end of the day for want of love
and no one notices her absence.

Lonelier even than loneliness itself
my soul melts like the wax on a burnt out candle
in the temple of my body.

Mila Sor

STAY CALM

Stay calm in the coming times,
still as a flower that only blooms at night,
as a moon asleep
on empty rooftops
with the bloodshot eyes of pain.

On the other side of a voice
hide yourself,
like a thought wrapped in fog,
like a line in an unread postcard
like a new letter in a word only spoken in a dream.

Stay calm
until the destiny changes course,
calm as a glance
that seeks and finds,
still as a window pane –
on the outside cold,
on the inside misted by sighs
and marked by someone's fingerprints.

THE ROAD OF SILK

A desert wind steals your touch
that wraps around my body
and weaves endless silk,
leaving me naked and vulnerable.

Somewhere an invisible door opens
and someone reaches out to me
wishing to cover me with the softness
of a slowly dying day.

But I can't stand, I can't stand the calmness of oases
and the falseness of mirages!
My eyes are in love with the redness of the sand
and the bloody skies,
for they keep imprints of the rises and falls of my love.
My eyes are in love
with the passionate touch of fingers entwined in the
dark,
and the eyes that say: You are the Sun
that sets my soul on fire.

I don't remember, I don't remember
when did I come barefoot on this road?
I don't recall your touch turning
into a road of silk, and my loneliness
becoming a caravan of sorrowful poetry.

See,
see how without a sound the sun dies
and sinks into a barren womb!
See how the wail of love,
muffled by desert silence, shatters my heart,
and my hands glue it back together
with the salt of my tears!

Who ordered the wind
to steal from me the talisman of your touch?
Who put the happy birds in a lonely cage?
Oh, gloomy days of darkness!
Oh, stolen smiles and flowers without bloom!
My arms
have no power to cover my nakedness.
My hands
are pleading to the wind
to return the softness of your touch.

MESSAGE

My thoughts float like dust particles
in an empty room.
I touch them with a finger,
they fade away.
I form them in speech,
and they echo.
In my chest, worlds are suffocating me,
buried under the ghosts of cutdown trees and smog.
I open the window to let in the light
that carries messages
from worlds thousands of years away.
One day, a hand will pull back the curtain
and snuff out the sun in my eyes.
The blazing fire will become a firefly lost in the night.
But until then, each new thought
will open a new horizon of existence.

Mila Sor

I HAVE BECOME YOU

My soul has nested on your chest like a seagull
for whom the sky is uncharted territory.
I have become you. I'm your shadow when you walk,
the burden of your pain when you sit,
I'm the salt in your tears,
the prayer on your lips,
every letter of every word you speak.
When passion floods your veins,
I'm the blood that soaks into your every atom
like water into thirsty earth.

I have become you.
I am born when the breath of dawn touches me
and turns me into the glimmer of your eyes.
I age in the shadow of your brow
and in the softness of your cheeks that treasure my every
touch
like a sacred imprint of a cross.
I have become you.

I HAVE EXISTED FOR CENTURIES

I see myself in the eye of Time.
From the whirlpool I sink down to the bottom,
then again I resurface.
I have existed for centuries, but no one knows me.
In the morning, I plant thoughts and wait for words to grow
to help me find myself when I get lost.
I hunt for sounds of wild animals
and I make a sacrifice to the gods
to gratify their hunger.
At every convent, I pray for the deer to have peace and quiet
when they drink water at the river
and for the ozone layer holes to disappear
so children can build their sand castles in peace.
I have done this for centuries, but no one knows me.

Mila Sor

THE SPACE BETWEEN TWO WORLDS

In the space between two worlds
is the union of our being.
There are no shadows,
for we hide the sun in our chests –
we shine to illuminate ourselves for each other.

We merge our hands to build walls around us,
and create a dream that will be our truth.
We read every thought in the eyes of each other,
as if from the handbook of love,
with every word spoken we write our history.

UNION

With our breath we create clouds
to hide the steps of our disobedient thoughts.
The union of our skies takes place unseen
like a sigh in the wind.
The spinning wheel of time
wraps centuries around its finger,
while we unwrap our cocoon before God,
praising His name with incense in hand
and the smell of basil.
In the holy dust, our souls
weighed down by desire for each other
will take root and like vines intertwined
will climb the wall
that separates us from eternity.

THE SUN WILL RISE

Hidden in the forest I hear the flowers weep.
Their tiny little heads looked for the sun all day long
and the clouds gathered like a dark procession
over the tops of the tallest trees.
The fields, heavy with the weight of seeds,
exhaled an autumn-scented breath.
What heights are those where the sky
is day and night tainted with bloody dew?
What land is that where the smell of unborn fruits
is only felt after the rain falls?

I can no longer be like a bird
sleeping with eyes open in a nest of thorns,
I can no longer sing
when my throat is choked from weeping.
My fate is a sky that narrows
to fit through a bottleneck.
My fate is a dream trapped in a bubble.

Wrapped in the shawl of loneliness
deep in the dark forest,
all day I listen to the flowers weeping
and the wind whispering to me: the sun will rise.

I DREAMT

I dreamt
that from the sweat filling the grooves on our foreheads
moons grew and directed harvests,
and caused the premature bloom of roses you picked for
me.
Rivers flowed into the lines of our palms,
and from them onward to the ocean of eternity.
I dreamt
that the spider web stretched between directions
was failing under the weight of time,
and the centuries were falling like snowflakes
into a bottomless universe.

Mila Sor

COGNITION

We're approaching the edge of cognition,
opening the cage door
to set the heart free.
Quiet prayers spoken from icy lips
like steam melt the snow
on bell towers of forgotten churches.
You are present everywhere –
in the silence of darkness,
in the talk of light,
in the alphabet of extinct language.
I am always absent
like the silence of light
like the talk of darkness,
like a nonexistent letter in an alphabet.

IN THE LONESOME GARDEN

You hide in the apple of love,
deep in the lonesome garden whose smell
gives birth to my desire to have you.
I'm a seeker of lost treasures
in labyrinths of trodden pathways
opening invisible doors looking for you.
In cracked rocks I find sparks
of days never born
and of nights never dawned upon,
and in the dust footprints of an angel with broken wings.

Are you a man or God, a shadow or real? -
I whisper sleepily in the night,
while combing my hair with the wind,
and covering my nakedness with a shirt of moonlight,
because I want to greet you like a goddess when I find you.

Mila Sor

IN SILENCE WE REMEMBER THE PAST

In silence, we remember the past
when sound was born from the rocks,
and the lakes slept in the eyes of lovers,
when fallen leaves adorned the wet asphalt,
and from the tear on the stone a flower grew,
when from the creases of the soul a bird flew
to places the wind had never been.

At night, I still hear the echo of your sighs
entangled in my hair
like seagulls nested in softness,
they refuse to be released.

In silence, we remember the past
when love, uninvited, followed after us.

TIME TOOK CARE OF EVERYTHING

Heavy as sin is the silence in the empty room.
At the doorstep, old tattered shoes
hide one-way roads,
and our names, lost in space,
have grown silent.
Time has taken care of things,
covered window panes with newspapers,
covered chairs and tables with white sheets,
covered keys and locks with rust.
Dampness found a home in the walls,
and grief in the eyes.
On the floor, shadows are layered upon shadows,
dust upon dust,
and love fills with new love the void in the heart.

Where are you?
Time has blurred the space between us,
feeding our eyes with haze and oblivion.
Chimney smoke has covered the clouds,
and the prayers we used to believe in
have changed their meaning.
Your photograph has turned to hourglass sand,
and the little fish has fallen asleep
on the bottom of the glass bowl,
far from her home.

FOR MY HOMELAND

While I pass through the present,
the past sticks to my feet
like the pollen of a trampled flower.
I know that the fragrance will awaken Time itself,
even before sunrise, and stir the tangled roots
under the dormant banner fluttering for centuries.
The sighs buried in our patriotic chests
still set the course of the wind.
When I stand over you while you sleep
I hold the same fear as our ancestors;
so every morning, in cups of red poppies,
I gather hope from the drainpipes of abandoned houses
and daydream of the return of all those who have departed.

FORGOTTEN

Like milk teeth, the walls of my home are wiggling;
I wait for them to fall, so that I can wrap up the pieces in a bun,
and throw them on the neighbors' roof.
Until then, I will peel off their paint with my fingernail,
layer by layer, and layer by layer,
I will discover the secrets of my ancestors.
I will shuffle truths on undiscovered roads,
I will hunt for embraces hidden in the mists of time.
Concealed glances I will release
like frightened does seeking new water springs,
and the light of souls departed
I will set them free from the weight of tombstones.
Like milk teeth, walls are wiggling
and I, leaning on them, will vanish
wrapped in secret, thrown upon the world's rooftop,
forgotten.

Mila Sor

CINDER

Your fingerprint
is in the melted wax of my heart.
In the darkness of a burnt-out candle
like a cinder it glows.

A WISH

They want me to walk the dark streets of life,
to vanish in the murky waters of swamps,
to grow like moss on heavy rocks,
and plant forest flowers into the cracked asphalt.
They want me to narrow the sky and bring it closer to the
earth,
so they can use the clouds to make dreamcatchers,
and catch birds in a single swipe of their hands.

But I want to plant flowers in your palms
and watch them grow from the softness of your skin,
I want to be a heavenly bird hidden in the sky of your eyes
tangled in the web of eternal love.
I want to overtake myself
with steps faster than my own shadow.

DON'T TAKE ME BACK

When I ran from myself
all roads were wiped from the world map.
There were no borders, just a desire overflowing
and nourishing the thirst in the heart.

Don't take me back when you see me running
over fields covered in drowsy flowers,
don't take me back when like a lonely leaf
I sail the waves of the wind to get to you.

I want to meet you at dawn,
to be the witness of the sun being born from your heart,
when a flock of birds flees your palms
to inhabit lonely parts of the world.

I ran from myself, and found myself in you.
You are my other self,
the self that's in love... that's in love,
like the grass in love with the touch of dew,
like the bee in love with the smell of the rose,
like the heart in love with love.

I ran from myself
and like a wild dove flew to your nest.
Don't take me back to the ruins,
don't take me back to where grief weighed down my wings,
where the ashes of an abandoned dream
wanted to become reality.